Old Clothes

New Trends

Making Vintage Modern

by Karen James-Welton

Introduction

Every year, around 80 billion garments are produced worldwide. When we purchase an item of clothing, we know little about who made it, how it was made and what the real cost is to the people who made them and to the environment.

Every one of our wardrobes is tainted. Seduced by fast fashion and having something new to wear at bargain prices. We have lost sight of the fact its production has brought working conditions to the developing world that were outlawed in Western countries a century ago.

Fashion should be fun – it should excite and inspire you. But definitely should not exploit the workers. Poor working conditions are not the only reasons for re-thinking how you shop. Its manufacturing is draining the planet's natural resources.

Cotton productions uses millions of gallons of water that is leaving vast areas of sea dried out. The toxic fumes created by the plastics used to produce many items is leaving whole villages uninhabitable.

We throw out tonnes of clothing that ends up in landfill when we get bored with wearing them. A survey for Oxfam and M&S found that one in 10 of us admitted to wearing just 10% of our wardrobe and estimated that there were 2.4 million garments hanging in our collective wardrobes.

We have a duty to future generations to think about what we are buying and really consider if we are purchasing out of need or desire.

If one million women bought their next item of clothing second-hand, we would save six-million kg of carbon pollution from entering the atmosphere.

Shopping second-hand and vintage will not only help to save the planet but will give you an individual look.

Buying clothes that don't harm the planet is becoming a higher priority – almost a fashion in itself.

Vintage clothing is having a bit of a moment – with vintage shops on every corner, websites selling "old" stuff worldwide. A few years ago, it was the likes of students and those into an alternative lifestyle that were buying it but now it has become more mainstream. With programmes such as Sex and the City, Kate Moss, Alexa Chung and other fashionista's wearing second hand clothes it has become another way of dressing – charity shops where old clothes once went to die are the "go to" shopping destination.

Sustainability is a word on everyone mind now and shopping second-hand is the new black and the next big thing.

As soon as long as I can remember I have had a passion for fashion – the styles, fabrics and patterns have always held a fascination for me. I wanted to wear the creations that I found in the pages of the glossy magazines that I spent my allowance on. But never having the budget to buy the designer pieces featured in the magazine I had to find another source for great clothes – so vintage was the answer.

I love mixing it up and creating my own individual looks – the vintage element means that I will never ever look the same as anyone else, as these pieces may make a nod to the trends are a one off one of a kind to die for items!!

Having worked in the fashion industry for many years I will always love the buzz I get when the new seasons trends are shown on the runways in New York, London, Milan and Paris. I have never been or never will be a slave to fashion but seeing how the designers incorporate the past into the collections, taking elements from history and creating something different but with a vintage twist is always exciting.

So, I am excited to bring you my style guide to making vintage part of your everyday wardrobe and share my passion for vintage clothing.

Even if it is something that you would never think of buying or wearing everyday – it can work for every occasion – how many times have you seen the same dress from the high street on someone else – never with vintage, each piece you buy will be a one off and totally individual. It is fabulous to be unique and find an outfit that no one else will have. You can get fabulous style without costing the earth in more ways than one!!

CHAPTER ONE

Why buy vintage?

Buying vintage means that you are buying a piece of history.

You will find the quality of fabric much better than now – clothes were not mass produced back then. To find the comparable quality in cloth and finish would be the equivalent of high-end high street or designer brands.

A beautifully cut wool suit from the 40's or 50's would cost around £175-200 from a vintage seller whereas designer brands would be at least 3 times that.

Imagine wearing a fitted 50's suit with a pussy bow blouse or sharp 60's shift to the office, a bias cut 30's dress to the Christmas ball, 70's sun dresses are very trendy but why buy one from the high street when you can have one off original. When everyone is lusting after the new "it bag" how cool would it be to own a totally one-off vintage one that no one has? There are so many ways that you can add a touch of vintage to your wardrobe.

Vintage shopping means you get more for your money – it doesn't necessarily mean cheap but with regards to fabric – vintage fabric offers many wonderful options that in today's age of mass manufacture would cost vast amounts of money to produce – you can choose from opulent silks, satins, lace, and brocades or fine wools and tweed, the softness of cashmere and cotton.

If there is one thing that separates those with genuinely cool personal style from those who just have big bank accounts is the ability to "thrift". To go into a department store and come out with a stunning ensemble is one thing but it's the next level to pull it off in your local vintage store, it takes a strong sense of self and a great eye to do vintage well and it is no surprise that some of the most stylish women we know count vintage items among their wardrobes most precious items. Just like any current season fashion item vintage can be a cheap thrill or a big-ticket designer item. Best of all it is about making it your own. You have got to hunt for it, fall in love with it and then style it up but making the extra effort will make all the difference to your look.

There are many misconceptions with vintage but vintage is for everyone so let me see if I can dispel them, ,..........................?

Vintage works on all shapes and sizes, ages and lifestyles. It just takes a little more time to find the style for you; in fact, I am certain that you will find very similar outfits that you would normally wear but it will be your own style and you are guaranteed never to be wearing the same dress as anyone else.

"Buy Less Choose Well Make it Last" - Vivienne Westwood

I can't wear vintage at my age:

Many women over 40 and beyond when asked about wearing vintage, most of them will say that it doesn't attract them as you can never be sure of sizing and trying on in a makeshift fitting room at a market stall or dusty old vintage doesn't hold much appeal so it is no surprise that the older woman is less inclined to strip down and pull on a vintage frock.

But at the end of the day many vintage pieces are classic styles, think of simple shift dresses, pencil skirts, well cut suits and cashmere sweaters so women of all ages can wear vintage.

If you take a look at the brands that are popular with 40+ women they are inspired by iconic pieces from the past. Vintage is a way of investing in classics that will be staples in your wardrobe that you bring out time after time.

The most common argument I hear is – it won't fit me. But is actually an older and curvier woman who is likely to unearth a gem at a bargain price.

Kerry Taylor of Kerry Taylor Auctions regularly sells lesser-known designer vintage pieces for under £100. "Larger sizes are often sold cheaper simply because they are harder to sell. Older women exclude themselves from the market" Kerry says "because they are of the mindset that vintage doesn't work on them but you can find pieces that will work on every shape and size". Think of a classic hourglass figure with hips and boobs, perfect for 40's and 50's suits.

Don't be afraid to have a piece altered to make it fit to your shape – better to be sustainable and give these beautiful pieces a new lease of life rather than sitting in a dusty shop.

Most women over 50 just can't fling on a vintage frock in the same way a 20 something could but with a bit of tailoring it can look amazing. And many vintage pieces are perfect for an older lady that needs a touch of coverage in the upper arm area – think of all of those glorious balloon and chiffon sleeves from the 1970's?

The other excuse I hear all the time is – it will make me look

frumpy or like my grandma. Designers draw inspiration from the past all the time and there are only so many ways that you can re-invent a frock therefore many vintage pieces are classic items that are always on trend – think of a navy blazer or a pussy bow blouse - study the trends and see where the influence has come from. Colour and texture are the first things to look for - you can't beat the intensity of vintage colours; look at the shapes next - 60's coats are the ultimate in chic when thrown over a pair of jeans, 70's shirt dresses are perfect for summer just add a pair of modern shoes or belt. Take a Chinese jacket or velvet opera coat from the 1920's that can be given a contemporary look. Try a classic pleated or A line skirt which are always all over the runway - every season shows some variation of it - wear it with a polo neck in winter paired with knee high boots or a simple white shirt and loafers in summer.

The key to making vintage look modern is mix it with contemporary pieces rather than wearing everything from the same era but don't get me wrong there are some fabulous 50 plus women who wear full on vintage every day and look amazing but for the majority of more mature women not looking as though you stepped out a BBC costume drama is the way to go!

Vintage jewellery is an excellent way to embrace the vintage trend. Statement pieces, layers of pearls a la Chanel who wore them in vast numbers right into her 70's, try an armful of vintage bangles - channel the extremely chic Iris Apfel or find a great pair of vintage chandelier earrings. Vintage silk scarves are a perfect option too - invest in a few that you can wear in so many way - in your hair, around your waist as a belt or just throw on around your neck for a pop of colour.

One advantage of buying vintage is the quality of the fabric and the way the garment is cut – you just don't get that with high-street pieces and as you get older it's all the more important that your clothes look and feel good. Think of it as investment shopping and to get the quality of fabric found in vintage clothing you are talking designer prices.

It's only for fancy dress and themed events - vintage offers flattering styles and modern trends. Everyday items – blazers, boots, scarves, pencil skirts, A line dresses and the LBD are all classic vintage styles that can be worn by everyone as part of their everyday wardrobe.

Not on trend

designers look to the past for inspiration and ideas for new styles and current trends so, what could be more fabulous than wearing the original inspiration behind the trend. It is a great way to get a designer look for half the cost and have an individual take on the runway styles. By reading the key trends and looking at the basic shapes, colours and which era is being showcased you can find vintage versions.

First and foremost, look at the colours that seem to be running through the collections – are they bright and bold or is one shade jumping out, are they more pastel and muted, or is the classic monochrome a feature?

Next take a look at the print – is it florals – are they small or large? Stripes – wide apart or narrow? Abstract shapes?

Focus on the cut – what is the key skirt length, is a straight or asymmetric. Trousers – cropped, or ankle length – wide leg or skinny? What are they being worn with – jackets or a shirt – is it tucked in or out?

Is there an influence from another era – the bias cut of the 1930's or the power suit from the 1980's or is the 70's vibe running through the collection?

Once you have all the key elements you can start to see how you can hunt for original items to that would work.

Accessories pay a major part in creating the look and for the runway Designers will add all sorts of mad pieces to create theatrics and dramas, so again you need to look at the basics.

Look at the shoes – what is the heel height – high, flat or kitten? What is the toe shape – rounded or pointed. Plain or decorative?

Move onto bags are they large or small – worn on the shoulder or hand held, look at the colours and prints on these too – this could be an easy way to switch your look up for the season without spending a fortune – and why not find a vintage version to give you an even more individual take on the new trend.

Vintage won't fit me – yes sizing can be difficult but once you find a style that is right for your shape you will be able to find pieces that work for your shape and there are always accessories – scarves, jewellery and why carry the latest "it bag" when you can have your own individual vintage one. Don't be afraid to buy a bigger size and have it tailored to fit.

CHAPTER 2

Vintage Essentials – making it modern.

Vintage items are just clothes at the end of the day and can be worn in exactly the same way as piece you would buy from high street stores, just because they are old makes no difference to where and how you can wear them.

Vintage Dresses – add a few different styles that you can wear for all occasions:

- A 60's shift – worn with a pair of opaque tights and a polo neck underneath will take to you work - wear it with a pair of knee-high boots or into the evening with a sweater and worn with a cute pair of heels.

- Floral 50's cotton frocks look great in the summer for weddings teamed with a cardigan or jacket, or wear them with flats for a more casual feel.

- Silky 30's tea dresses work perfectly for summer days.

- Maxi dresses teamed with strappy flats and a floppy hat for picnics and days at the beach.

Jackets – vintage jackets can work in so many ways:

- Denim jackets look great worn over summer dresses or teamed with cute cotton skirts.

- Worn in leather works with dresses too giving it the "pretty v tough" feel.

- Suit jackets or a Chanel style tweed jacket or an oversized blazer can dress up a pair of jeans – worn with heels or flats.

- Fur – real or faux will add a touch of glamour to any outfit.

- A sparkly evening jacket works well for daytime too over a wool skirt or pair of trousers and jeans.

Skirts – wear with boots, a pair of flats or killer heels:

- Very on trend but very flattering on all body shapes is a fabulous midi skirt – take one from the 50's in a print or a wool 70's one for winter warmth.

- A pencil skirt is perfect for the office with a cute cardi or pussy-bow blouse.

- Wear a 60's mini if you have the legs for it or add a pair of opaques in winter.

  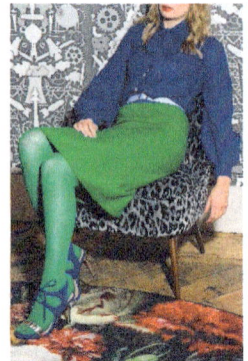

Jewellery – build up a collection of costume pieces that will add instant bling to an outfit:

- Brooches can be worn high on the shoulder to bring light to the face, wrap a cardigan around your waist and fasten with a big stone, add one to waist of a dress or to a simple wool hat.

- Cuffs are great to add a statement to any outfit – buy them in lots of colours and styles and wear a few together.

- Vintage necklaces to add impact to a simple white shirt or polo neck sweater.

My top ten pieces that everyone should have in their wardrobe. Build these items into your wardrobe and you will be able to create lots of different outfits with just a few items.

A suit – why?

Because it is such a classic, it can be worn in so many ways, you have two items for the price of one – choose skirt suit or trousers whichever you prefer and whether you go for a neutral shade or go bold is your choice. Finding great suits isn't easy but be patient the right one will come your way – go for classic tailoring and it will take you anywhere.

A great blazer – why?

It will be one of the most useful items you ever buy, go for a classic oversized style that can be worn with everything – go for a neutral shade to start off with or go for a plaid or check – don't rule out the men's section to get the oversize feel.

Denim jeans and jacket – why?

OK, that is essentially two items but if you can find both that is fabulous – vintage jeans are the best fit, already worn in and in the softest denim with no impact on the planet – my go to have always been Levi 501 but find your style and shape to best fit you, a denim jacket will go with everything – do double denim or throw it on over a summer frock, dress down a smart skirt or dress – go for a quality denim in a neat style that will work with everything.

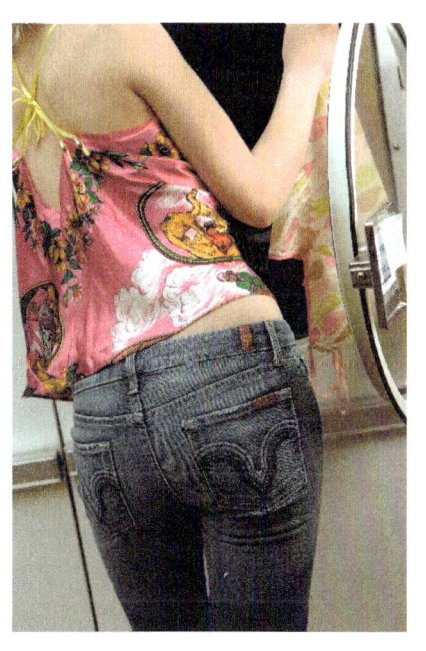

Every day dress – why?

This will be your best friend – your go to item you can dress it up or down for any occasion. What to go for – that is up to you – what shapes do you like? My favourite style is shirt dress that can be worn for every season layered up over sweaters and blouses or under jackets and cardigans.

Every day dress – why?

This will be your best friend – your go to item you can dress it up or down for any occasion. What to go for – that is up to you – what shapes do you like? My favourite style is shirt dress that can be worn for every season layered up over sweaters and blouses or under jackets and cardigans.

High waisted trousers - why?

The 80s classic will work day or night, every season and become a wardrobe staple. Pick a pair in a fabulous check or bold bright and wear with a simple t shirt or a pussy bow blouse, add in your blazer and you are set.

Midi skirt - why?

It is so flattering for any shape, it is classic that will take you anywhere, dress it up or dress it down – wear it with trainers or heels. You can find them pleated or plain, printed or flouncy whatever you choose you can't go wrong.

Just as long as it hits your mid-calf so below the knee.

A great coat - why? Second-hand coats are always such great quality and you can just throw them on, over whatever you have on and feel instantly dressed up. Choose a fabulous classic wool or a trench belted at the waist or a real or faux fur or maybe a butter soft leather one and why stop at one give yourself some options.

Shirt or blouse - why? Your top is what will make or break your outfit so go for a simple button-down shirt or a classic blouse in a beautiful fabric or print or go for a full-on flounce with an 80s pussy-bow.

Statement or graphic t-shirt - why? What is easier than a T-shirt? – nothing and a vintage print t-shirt is a must have. Think of your favourite band, a cartoon character or whatever grabs your attention. Wear with your jeans, a midi skirt or layered under a strappy dress or take a leaf out of Carrie Bradshaw's book and wear it in the evening with a glitzy skirt and accessories.

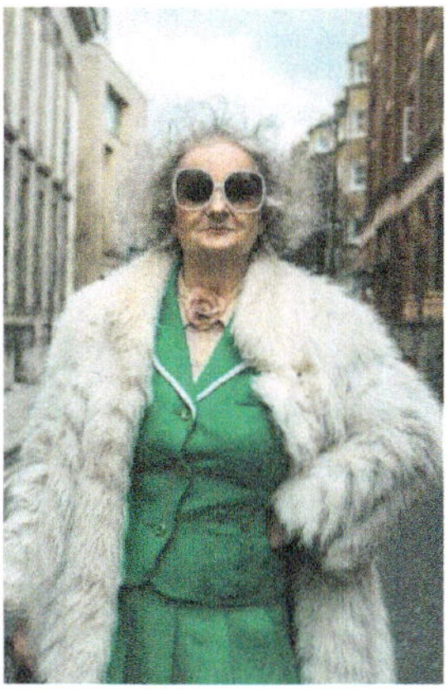

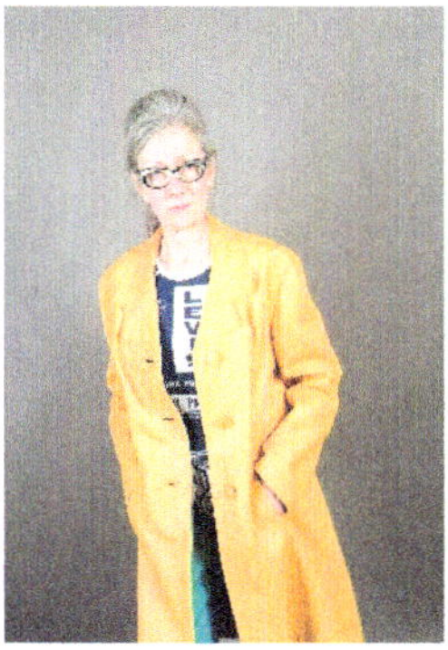

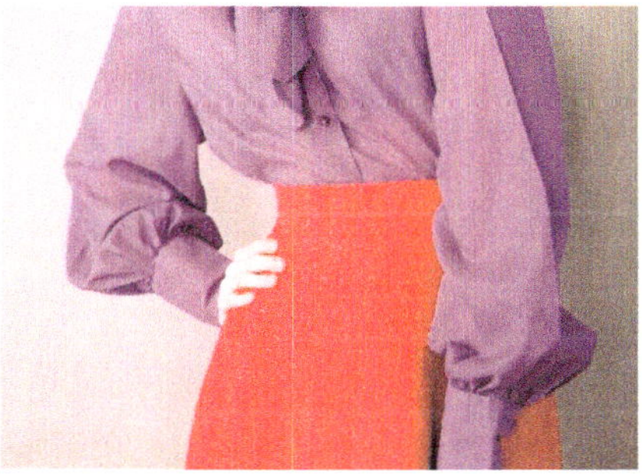

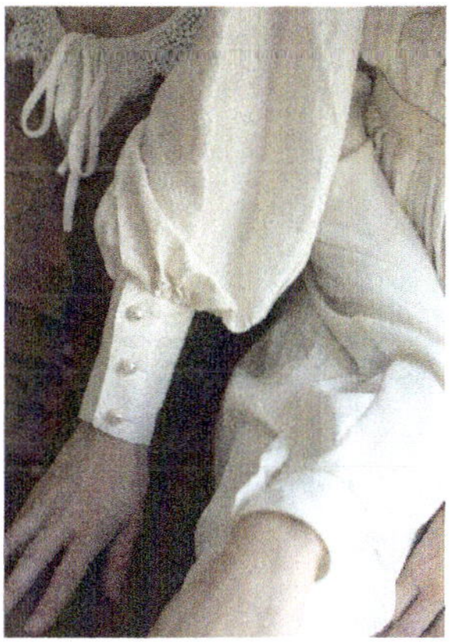

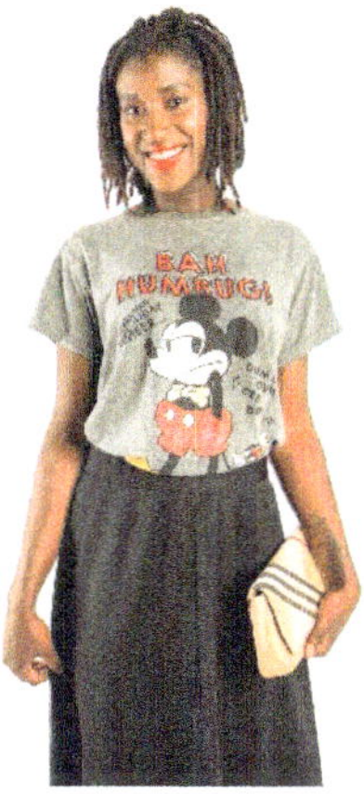

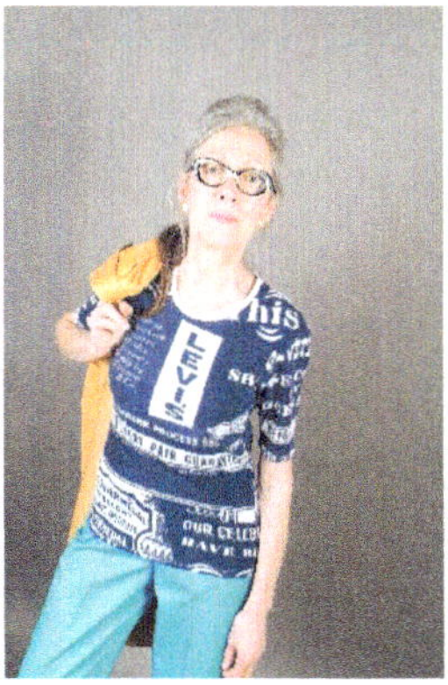
LEVI'S

One totally OTT item – why? Why not!? There is always that one piece that is so fabulous you just have to have. It may be a brocade dress or a stunning coat or full-on glam dress.

Don't leave it for an occasion to bring her out, for date night, drinks with the girls – it will make you feel like a movie star. G for whatever takes your fancy and wear it with a flourish.

CHAPTER 3

How to wear - COLOUR

Vintage clothing is all about colour. Colours were much brighter and bolder – think fabulous floral 50s prints or soft pastels from the 1930s or who can forget the opt art 60s and 70s shades of orange and brown.

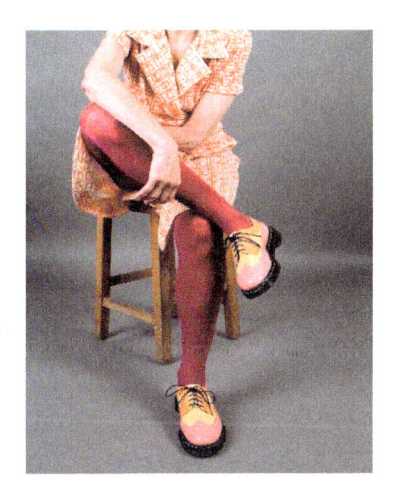

Or you can't forget the neon's in the 80's and early 90's!! Full on bright can be scary and takes guts to pull off but you can always add a neutral such as camel or grey to tone it down.

Think of ways to add colour to your outfits – navy and red or pink work well or try a yellow with grey. Mix camel with any colour and it adds another dimension. If you think of the colour wheel – opposites will always work together or if that is all too scary then add a pop of colour with accessories – a bag or bold necklace or a fabulous pair of shoes in a bright colour.

TEXTURE – think brocades, plaid, lace, butter soft leather, chunky knits, boucle wool or suede and silks – don't be afraid to mix them up – wear a chunky knit over a silk slip dress add in a pair of DMs or trainers for a funky modern twist.

Why save metallics or sequins for evening add them to your day wear – a sparkly jacket over your jeans or wear an evening skirt with your t shirt and denim jacket.

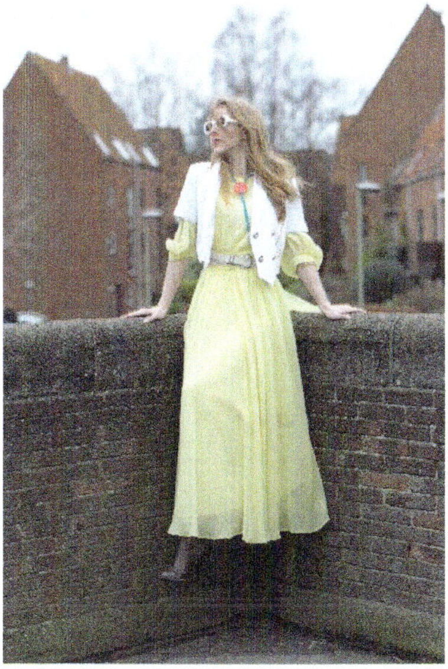

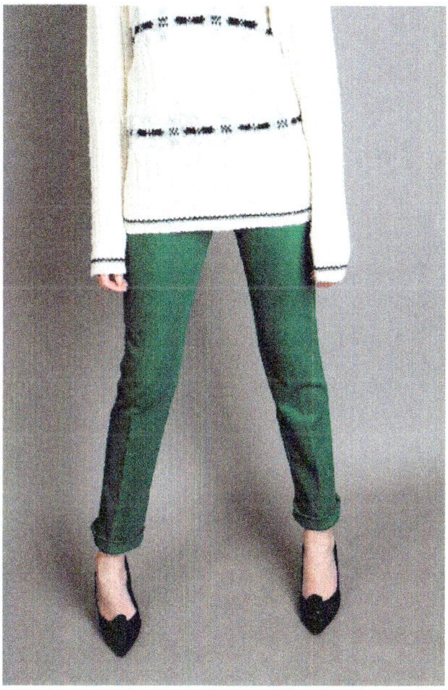

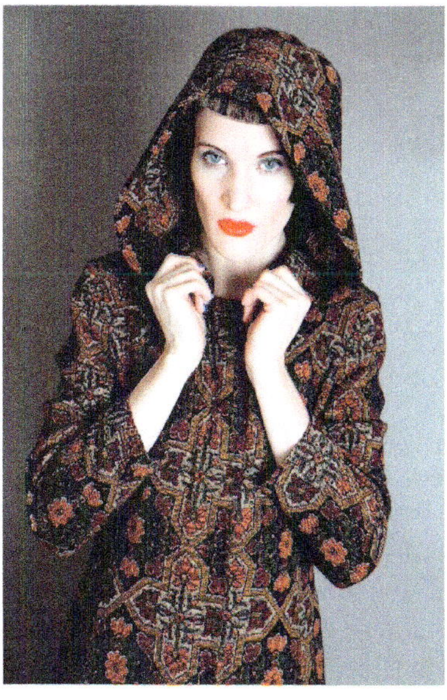

PATTERN AND PRINT – vintage prints are the best and although it involves nothing more than putting two items on together many people feel intimidated by mixing prints.

It may be a bit of a gamble but once you have figured it out there are so many options.

The trick is about finding the common denominator through colour and making sure the scale and size are well balanced.

Mixing prints in different colour families can seem a bit wacky but as long as there is a single colour that travels though both it will work.

You can always anchor with denim which is a great neutral and above all trust your gut.

At the end of the day if you love it that is all that matters!!

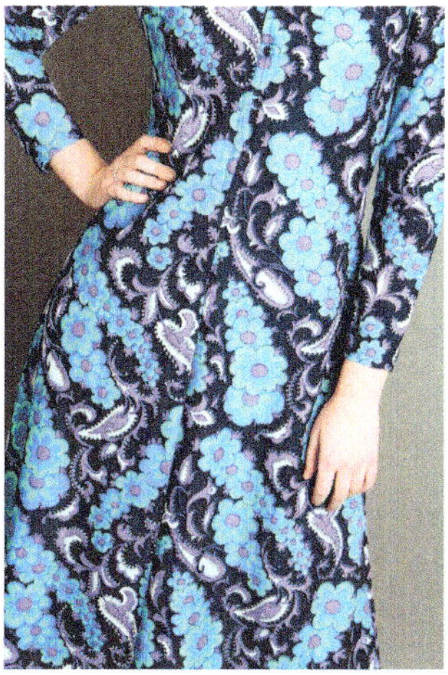

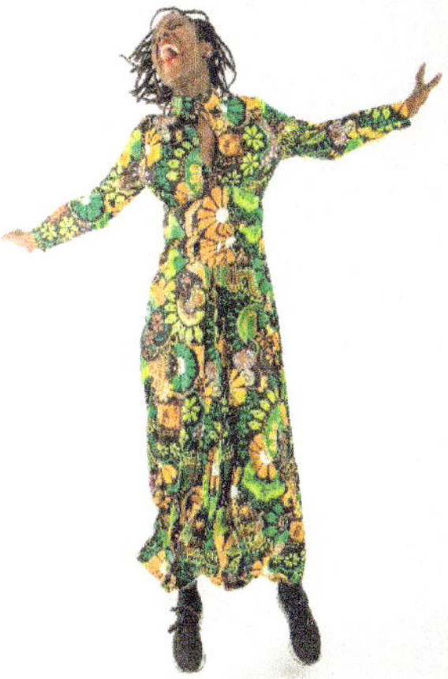

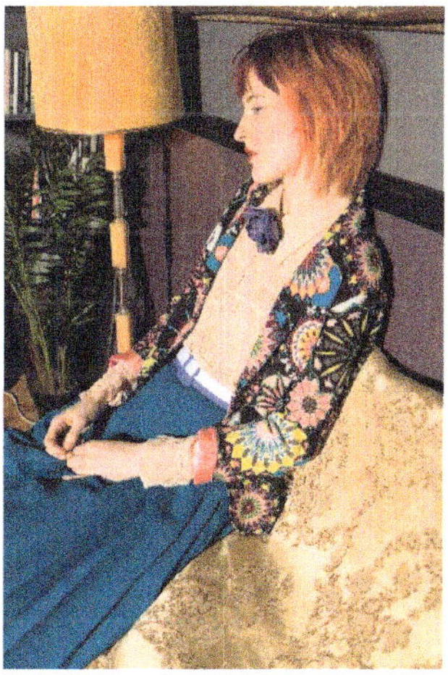

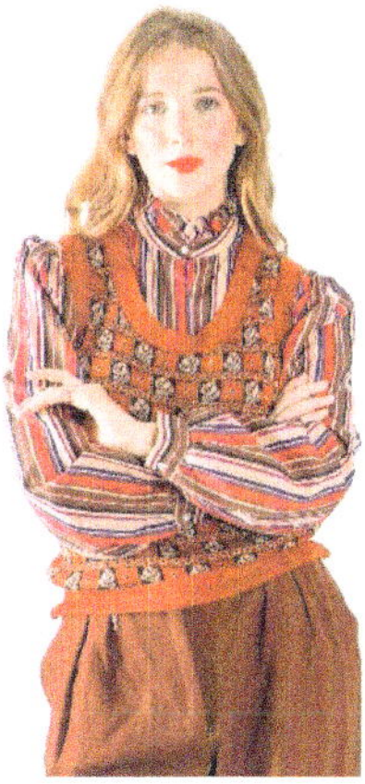

CHAPTER 4

Accessories

Vintage accessories are an easy way to start your vintage journey if you are not used to buying this way.

Handbags

Why have the latest "it bag" when you can buy a much better made individual vintage one. Bags come in so many shapes, sizes and fabrics so have a collection that you can mix up with your outfits.

Hunt for classic shapes like a Hermes Kelly or Birkin – they don't have to be designer ones, just go for quality leather and finish.

Collect various fabrics such as tapestry or beaded and satin clutches for evening wear or for summer find a pretty straw one that you can take to the beach.

42

Scarves

Such a great way to add a touch of colour to your wardrobe, you can pick up vintage scarves for next to nothing and there are so many ways that you can wear them.

- Tie them in a big bow in your hair, or round a loose pony tail.

- Take a leaf from Gucci who for a number of seasons have shown bold head scarves tied over the hair and at the back of the neck.

- Around your neck in a simple loop or tie it in a bow, fold it into a triangle and tie at the back – there are so many ways to tie it.

- Wrap a small square around your wrist as a bracelet.

- Use a long scarf as a belt around your jeans.

- Make a jacket by tying the corners of a large square to make an oblong and pop your arms through the holes to wear as a jacket.

- Add a scarf to your bag to give it a whole new look.

- Gather all the ends together and tie in a knot to give you a great summer bag.

Glasses and sunglasses

When you have to wear glasses why not go for an individual pair of lenses. There are lots of companies that sell vintage frames or can put your prescription into other frames.

With the trend for over-sized sunglasses go for a great pair of vintage ones, you can pick up original ones on Ebay for not very much as well as designer pairs.

Think Jackie O with her over-sized sunnies or Carrie Bradshaw's aviators.

Jewellery

Build up a collection of statement vintage jewellery that will add some bling to your outfits.

Brooches are perfect for taking outfits to the next level and can be picked up really reasonably from charity and vintage shops.

- Pop one at the collar of your shirt
- Instead of buttoning your cardigan wrap it around and secure with a brooch instead
- Add a couple to the shoulder of your evening dressing
- Wear one at the waist instead of a belt
- Pin one on the collar of your jacket
- Add one to the brim of your hat or beret

Necklaces

- Layer up the pearls Chanel style

- Lots of gold chains can work with a classic white shirt or polo neck

- Statement diamante for evening with your little black dress

Bangles and bracelets

- Add an armful of bangles for a Bohemian feel

- A statement cuff can look great with a ¾ length sleeve

Earrings

Easy to find and in so many different styles, a great way to add some glamour for day and night:

- Over the top chandelier earrings can dress up any outfit

- Simple pearls will be a classic addition

- 80s gold clip-ons can be found easily and will instantly dress up an outfit or how about a pair of pretty 50s floral ones to add a touch of floral chic for Spring.

Hats

From berets to fedoras, floppy straw hats for summer picnics, formal hats for smart weddings. There are so many options.

Berets are so easy to wear – very Parisian chic and practical in the winter to keep your head warm.

Straw hats look amazing in the summer with a simple maxi dress and perfect for giving you some shade in the sun.

Cocktail hats and 80's ones with veils have made a comeback recently and were seen on the runway from Gucci and other designers.

A trilby the menswear classic that looks great on girls too. Tweed flat-caps can look great worn with jeans and an over-sized jacket – perfect for bad hair days!!

Shoes

Some people may not like the thought of literally walking in someone else's shoes but you can very often pick up amazing pairs of hardly worn shoes. Dead-stock which are items that have normally come out of a closing down shop and have never been worn.

You can always clean inside with a baby wipe and put in an insole.

- Loafers are always a great buy – wear them with jeans, or coloured tights and a midi skirt

- Boots are great to buy vintage – go for an ankle boot in a bright colour or a slouchy 80's pair to wear with your day dress or skirt or there is nothing better than a pair of vintage cowboy boots

- Courts with a classic heel will always be an investment will dress up any outfit. You often find 80s courts with great detailing and a little bit unusual

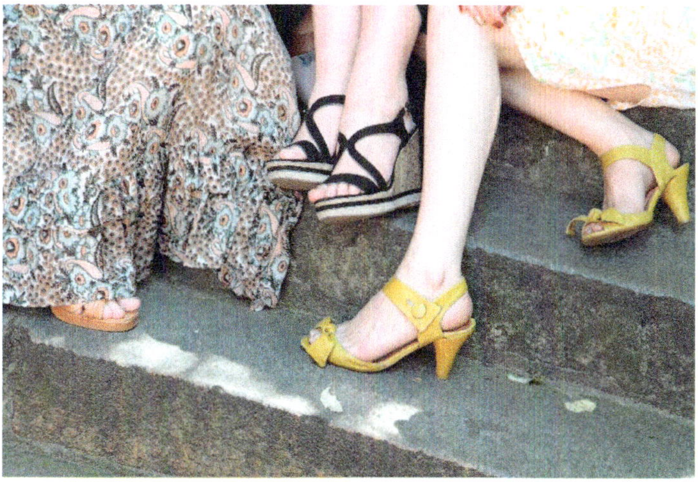

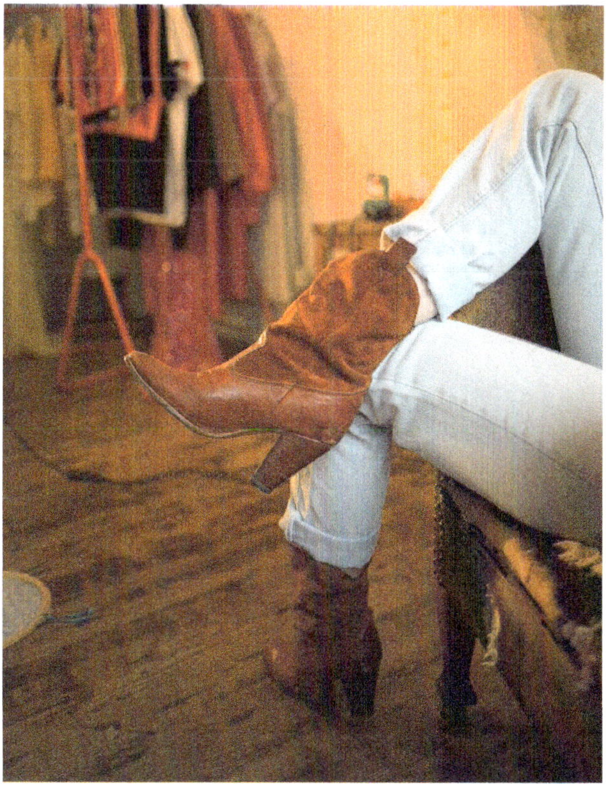

CHAPTER 5

Girls who do vintage

There are so many vintage loving ladies out there that love mixing up their wardrobe with vintage, so in the following chapter I thought I would share with you a few of the stylish slow fashion advocates that I am loving right now, along with some style icons past and present to give you some inspiration to start your vintage journey.

Mia – @Mad 70s

I have always enjoyed wearing unique outfits and the only way of pulling that off, is to invest in unique vintage pieces. Charity shopping is just fun - you get to find some real gems amongst rails and rails of clothing. Its affordable and you are giving the piece a life and home. I've always said 'One man's trash, is another man's treasure.

I also choose to buy vintage and charity because it's less damaging to our planet and I'd like to believe choosing to buy sustainable fashion would help others to do so as well.

I've always been influenced by 60's and 70's music - I used to stick the covers of my dad's records on my wall, which was my inspiration to get dressed in the morning; This included covers of the Beatles, David Bowie, Rolling Stones, some 80's (Debbie Harry of course).

I also grew up in a small town, Worcester, outside Cape Town (South Africa) where clothing was minimal and choices of shops were limited. It frustrated me when I wore the same piece/outfit as my friend, so I decided I will only buy clothing where no one else is buying from, which was the only Salvation Army in town, with the BEST pieces; 50's tennis dresses with cut out detail, linen two-piece suits and so much more!

Beth Jones – @Bjonestyle

I love the uniqueness of items. I love the hunt and finding pieces and how one piece can inspire a whole bunch of ideas. It's my therapy, my creative outlet and makes me happy.

Kayt Mendies – @City Thrifter

I always had a unique style. I was always drawn to vintage and second-hand because I was able to create outfits that nobody else had and build a wardrobe with diversity. I love mixing decades and the history of pieces. I get a buzz from vintage and second-hand shopping that in my opinion you just don't get from the high-street. I have so many pieces that I love and wear over and over in many different ways.

Rebbeca Weef Smith – @rebeccaweefsmith @The Happy Dresser.

I've never gone out thrift or vintage shopping with a particular piece in mind however, I do have a digital mood board on my phone with ideas for the way I want to dress in the coming few weeks. I find that just having that as a style guide in my head means I'm drawn to items which fit the look I'm after.

I hardly ever try on, but if you aren't confident with judging fit, have your measurements to hand and a tape measure in your bag. Sizes from the past do not correspond to modern day sizing. I would never bother with any size label, I have clothes in my wardrobe ranging from a 6 to an 18, they all fit.

If you truly love a piece and have the funds to buy, then do. I have regretted the ones that got away more than I've ever regretted a purchase. There is rarely a second chance with a really good old garment. It will be gone when you go back to the store. Sometimes I've fallen in love with a fabric but not a shape and really wished I'd bought the piece to remake. Great vintage printed textiles can be unpicked and reworked. Converting second-hand is my number one best way to create unique garments. You don't have to look *vintage* to adore pre-loved pieces.

Cameron Silver Decades – taken from a quote in A to Zoe by Rachel Zoe

Ask yourself when you look at a vintage piece, does it look modern? If it looks too vintage it can look costumery but even an Edwardian piece can have a modern feel.

Just because it has a label, it doesn't mean it is good.

A vintage piece has to have good design and it has to be wearable.

Vintage accessories can transform your outfit, you can wear the same little black dress over and over by changing the accessories.

Unless you are a hardcore collector, buy vintage that you can wear not archive. Buy clothes that have a little history and mystery.

Make it modern through the mix, for example a 50s dress with a pair of modern shoes and lots of bling.

Caroline – @Knickers Models Own

Why I love vintage so much? I think it's holding history in my hands. Looking at a garment or an accessory and imagining its previous life, its beginnings, each with its own story. Where has it been? What was its purpose? Why has the chapter ended? Charity shops are rich with vintage pieces, very often the label and the small sizing the clue. I'm also as fascinated with the detailing: a carved button, the rolled edge of a silk scarf, the hand stitched lining of a tweed coat. My style take on things?

Mix up your decades, you won't look back.

Kerry Curl – Award-wining Photographer and second-hand fashion advocate @kerrycurl

As a photographer, a by-product of the way I create my images is that I often find myself working with pre-loved, vintage, sustainable clothing. Given my interest over the years in second-hand shopping it's not surprising I found myself on this path. The work I tend to make reflects my own interest in style and history and is a way of communicating ideas that photography involving 'fashion' can be thoughtful and not just a vessel to shout 'sell sell sell' and 'buy buy buy!'

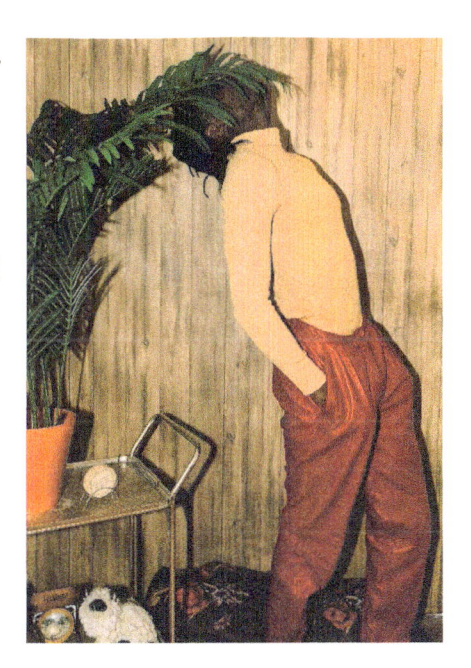

Disclaimer – my own adventures into second-hand fashion was originally down to economic necessity. It would be disingenuous of me to say that I began wearing second-hand or vintage because I was a super cool teenager of the 90s wanting to buck the mainstream.

The first second-hand thing I bought was a 70s gents blazer when I was 15. I wanted a blazer and that was the only way I could afford one.

It was embarrassing back then to be a kid who couldn't regularly buy new clothes. Thankfully attitudes have changed a lot in the last couple of years.

It's taken me years to get good at shopping second-hand but the more you do it the easier it becomes. I'm not a 100% second-hand shopper, I'd estimate about 30% of what I buy is new, but I'm trying really hard to make every purchase count. That's the beauty of taking a thoughtful approach to curating your wardrobe you don't have to dress head-to-toe in only vintage or preloved clothing to be part of this ever-evolving circular fashion conversation.

Second-hand fashion exists because people give away or sell what they no longer want. The reality is we are human and we all fall in and out of love with clothing regardless of whether we bought it new or second-hand. Our bodies change, our tastes change...we stop enjoying wearing things. Regardless of how old or how new the clothes we purchase are, if we *try* to make thoughtful purchases then that's a good place to start. Importantly let's be prepared to pass on what we no longer want by putting it into someone else's wardrobe thus extending the life of that piece of clothing. I love second-hand clothing because I get to practice what I preach which is using what's already produced. I always ask myself, "Why spend so much money buying a new look that just came back from the 1980's (now in poorer quality) when I can buy an original from a vintage store at a bargain?"

I personally think secondhand shopping is a recycle system that helps everyone involved in the process. The giver who reduced landfill waste, the buyer who finds pre-loved items at a bargain and in most cases, the charity organisations that receive donations from most second-hand stores.

"Fast Fashion isn't free someone is paying" - Lucy Siegle, Journalist and author.

Lauren Bravo – Author of Breaking up with Fast Fashion

I was wearing vintage long before we called it that. I grew up on charity shops, partly through thrifty necessity and partly through a passion for relics of the past that both my parents have instilled in me (I mean secondhand clothes and objects, not them). I was always obsessed with style from previous decades, poring over old 70s Jackie annuals when I was a kid and then getting heavily into vintage in my teens during the early days of eBay. I've always been massively sentimental about old things, and there was something about the thrill of clothes with history sewn into their seams that I found so much more attractive than whatever my classmates were wearing fresh off the rails at Topshop. I loved the theatrics of it, and thinking about who might have worn each piece before me. But if I'm honest the main appeal was the classic motivation of every adolescent: I thought it made me cool.

In my 20s I got more and more into fast fashion, though even when I was hitting the high street hardest, I still loved a bit of vintage. I pilfered coats from my grandmothers' wardrobes, which became staples for their emotional value as well as their quality design, and never stopped trawling charity shops for bargains. But it wasn't until I quit fast fashion a few years ago that vintage really came into its own again, as I realised that I'd been wasting so much money, time and energy on fleeting high street trends that fell apart after a couple of washes, when what I really wanted to be wearing was clothes that made me feel like I was back in those Jackie annuals. These days I like to think I show vintage the respect it deserves. I buy much more discriminately than I used to, taking the time to consider the purpose a garment will serve in my wardrobe rather than snapping up anything because it's cheap and I wait to find really special pieces that fit me, too, instead of squeezing myself into dresses I can't breathe in (60s shifts will never be a friend to my boobs) or badly altering larger items that should be left for a more deserving shopper. I know my spiritual era (late 60s to mid-70s, with serious Stevie Nicks) but I like to mix up classic vintage with newer pieces, like layering a balloon-sleeved maxi over a casual rollneck or teaming a floaty prairie dress with 90s trainers. And some of the better pieces from my old teenage archive are still going strong!

One of the most important tips is to know your measurements, and always ignore sizes on labels as these have changed wildly over the decades. Another big advantage when vintage shopping is having sewing skills or a good seamstress on call. If you're prepared to have things tweaked and altered to fit perfectly, it really broadens your horizons. I often take up maxi dresses by a few inches so they feel more wearable for the daytime, or remove shoulder pads so that 80s dresses feel more contemporary. When browsing take your time, vintage shopping should be a leisurely pleasure, not a grab-and-dash. Always browse every rail twice if you can, as for some reason the real treasures never seem to materialise on the first-time round. Don't be put off by a few musty aromas, they're much easier to get out than you'd think. My secret weapon is a soak in white vinegar solution, followed by a lengthy hang on an outdoor clothes line. But do pay careful attention to stains, flaws and really baked-in BO, as there's nothing more heart-breaking than getting a new buy home to discover a big hole or mark you hadn't spotted in the shop.

Finally, be prepared to leave empty-handed. While the frustration of vintage shopping can be that there's only one of each item, that's the beauty of it too, unlike fast fashion, with its never-ending conveyor belt of options, a great vintage find feels like a rare and precious thing. Fate is your stylist and destiny is your personal shopper.

Fate is your stylist and destiny is your personal shopper.

Not every shopping trip or Ebay session will be fruitful, and that's fine. Because when you do find something you adore, that fits like a glove, it feels as though it's meant to be yours.

Brenda Shop Bemuse

My vintage love affair began accidentally some years ago when I was on a training course and I popped into a charity shop that was next door to the bakery I bought my lunch from. I was just killing time before I had to get back, so I went in to browse. This was my first time in a charity shop! I fell in love with two amazing coats and bought them immediately! I had no idea they were vintage but they were absolutely gorgeous and I knew I had not seen anyone wearing this exact style.

The very first time I wore one of the coats, I was approached by a modelling agent! I was scouted on the spot and when I asked what caught his attraction, he said it was me in my coat!

One particular time, I was asked where I bought my coat from, and I was too embarrassed to say I had bought it from a charity shop, so I said it was a gift. The person commented that they had never seen one like this before and was going to try and find a similar style from the high street brands.

This made me take a closer look at the label and do some research because I really did not know where this coat was from! It was after this, that I came to understand that my coat was vintage, from the 1970's! There was no chance that person was going to find my coat on the high street! I loved my coat even more because I had something rare that others would not have.

My passion for vintage is driven by the uniqueness and scarcity of the pieces and I thoroughly enjoy styling vintage in a modern and fashionable way.

Knowing what I'm wearing is an authentic reflection from a former fashion era that can only be mimicked by today's designers and brands, gives me such a confidence boost because my style cannot be cloned like the rest of the fast fashion lovers who are wearing what the next person is wearing straight off the mass production conveyor belt!

As a beginner, I would suggest starting by visiting a vintage shop (so you know everything is vintage, making it easier to identify and eliminate the guesswork) and taking your time looking through the options. This way you can feel and try on the pieces and ask questions before making a commitment to purchase.

Choosing one or two key pieces you absolutely love and know you will wear again and again. Choose items that are versatile to wear, classic styles and season-less; in doing so, you will optimise how many ways you can style the piece, making each style look brand new.

Stick to colours, silhouettes and categories you are used to wearing. As you become more adept at shopping vintage you can explore outside of your comfort zone, but my advice in the beginning is to play it safe as the goal is to wear your vintage as often as you wear your non-vintage, so this should be a comfortable and familiar style to you.

My best tip on how to wear vintage is to wear your pieces exactly as you would the other items in your wardrobe.

There are no rules or mistakes in dressing up, so style yourself however you want to!

"I have always loved fashion so much and didn't have the access to the fashion I wanted so I would do vintage shopping" - Rachel Roy, Fashion Designer.

@belindasmetena Sustainable Fashion Advocate

I love second-hand clothing because I get to practice what I preach which is using what's already produced. I always ask myself, "Why spend so much money buying a new look that just came back from the 1980's (now in poorer quality) when I can buy an original from a vintage store at a bargain?"

I personally think secondhand shopping is a recycle system that helps everyone involved in the process. The giver who reduced landfill waste, the buyer who finds pre-loved items at a bargain and in most cases, the charity organisations that receive donations from most second-hand store.

Instagram is full of inspiration from accounts that share their passion for vintage – check out some of my favourites to get you started:

@bjonesstyle

@mamma_see_mamma_do

@affectionatelyaudrey

@athriftedwardrobe

@emsladeedmonson

Another great source of inspiration are the style icons from the past, celebrities and movie stars.

Jackie O – from the classic Chanel suit in the 60s to the oversized sunnies and 70s safari jackets, flares and trench her look will always be in style.

Lesser known is one of the four "swan" socialites singled out by writer Truman Capote is Slim Keith – what she wore we call basic wardrobe essentials today her style is considered as sporty elegance and the perfect capsule wardrobe.

Anita Pellenberg, Jane Birken who in the 70's inspired a generation with their relaxed laid-back style with over-sized blazers, simple shirts and jeans or dressing it up in a boho maxi – the look is still around today with designers like Chloe and Celine reinventing their look.

Over the years there have been a number of "IT GIRLS" that have had an impact on our style – Edie Sedgwick gave us black opaque tights and a love for antique earrings, more recently Chloe Sevigny has a style of her own mixing vintage and couture on the red carpet making her stand out from the crowd and who can forget Kate Moss the ultimate vintage style queen who has been at the fore front of making second-hand clothes the new must have.

Coco Chanel – who broke the rules when it came to dressing women with her designs, borrowing from her lovers' wardrobe with comfortable pants, the loose-fitting tweed jacket freeing women from the restraints of the corset and the look is still copied to day. Her signature boucle jacket are really easy pieces to find in second-hand and charity shops.

Carrie Bradshaw's style on Sex and the City brought vintage to a whole new generation, with her individual way of dressing mixing thrift shop finds and her unique way of putting the unexpected together.

My top tip for finding your vintage style is to create a mood board on say Pinterest or the old-fashioned way with tear sheets and scrapbook of the outfits you love then see what vintage pieces you can find to re-create the looks.

"Fast fashion is like fast food. After the sugar rush it just leaves a bad taste in your mouth." - Liva Firth, Ethical fashion advocate and founder of Eco-age.

CHAPTER 6

Handy hints on buying vintage

Shopping for vintage and second-hand takes more time and it not as easy as popping into the high-street and picking up whatever you want in your size, you have to make a decision there and then as it is a one-off piece and if you hesitate too long it will be gone. There are still pieces that I didn't buy that haunt me!! There will be times when you come away with nothing but right piece will always find you.

- Dress in garments that are easy to get out of; something you can slip on and off without fuss – my favourite uniform for vintage shopping is a button-down dress.

- Wear minimal make-up. Many vintage garments do up at the side and have to go over your head, rather than over your hips, so whilst it's tempting to don red lippy to get into the spirit of things, it's best not to smear it all over the neck of a pastel 50s frock. You won't be judged in a shop for not looking the part. Take a belt so you can cinch in the waist of items that are a bit big.

- Keep an open mind when you are shopping – that is the joy of vintage shops you never know what you will find!! Don't go with set pieces in mind but with an inspiration in your head and then see what takes your fancy. I tell my clients to put together a mood board on Pinterest or saved to their Instagram so they can keep track of what they are looking for.

- Look at the fastenings. Double-check that none of the buttons are missing and the zips are working properly. This may seem like a no-brainer, but all too often I've gotten home only to discover that a crucial covered button has fallen off or a zip is faulty. I always make a point of checking the buttons when I get the item home and making sure they are securing stitched – there is nothing worse than losing one when you are wearing it and not being able to replace it. Key areas to check fastenings are around the neck line where small buttons may be hidden under a collar, and also around the cuffs. Whilst you are there, make sure the belt is still attached. If there are belt loops and no belt, it's OK to ask for a small discount because the garment is no longer complete.

- Always check the armpits. Before the days of deodorant, sweat had a habit of damaging fabric due to the acidic qualities of perspiration.

- Have you noticed how dark vintage shops can be? Well, it's not always intentional (they can just be cluttered places), but it sure does make it harder to spot flaws. Hold it up to the light, you can instantly see any holes or repairs. The light will also shine through any patches where the fabric has become too thin and delicate. With woollen garments, check the elbows to make sure there is not excessive wear. But don't feel tempted to throw away a much-loved vintage sweater when it becomes worn, it can easily be patched and give it a whole new look and lease of life.

- Ignore the sizes – vintage isn't the same sizing as modern-day items so take a tape measure and know your measurements and use that as your guide.

- Talk to the sales assistants Don't be too proud to ask for advice in a shop, especially if you are looking for era-specific garments. This will speed up the learning process and before long you will be having a friendly debate on the age of a frock. Good shopkeepers should know their stock inside out and quite often they will keep special pieces behind for the right customer. It's also good to develop a relationship with the vendor, as they will start to look out for garments in your size and style. Most vintage sellers are passionate about what they do and are happy to talk to customers about stock, sizes and fair pricing.

- Always check the bottom of shoes. More often than not, a heel tip will be missing. Check the leather around the buckle and strap for signs of wear and tear. If a leather strap looks cracked, it may break off easily. Make sure the shoe is not too bendy and will hold your weight – this can be achieved only by trying it on. In some cases, the shoe's sole can be reinforced, but this can be costly.

- Avoid shoes where the leather has stiffened, as they will be uncomfortable to wear. If you love a pair but not sure about the colour, shoes can be dyed every colour under the sun!! Check out Affectionately Audrey on Instagram she is the queen of the shoe dye.

- Don't be tempted by garments that need altering above and beyond a simple strap shortening or a dropped hem. Alteration shops will do it justice and if the fabric is raw, frayed or thin, it may not last even one cold wash! But do get to know an amazing dressmaker as they can work miracles!!

- Try everything on. If you like it on the hanger, then chances are you will like it on you, but you also shouldn't shy away from the bizarre; sometimes a hanger can't convey an item's true potential, so get it on your body – what's the worst that could happen? As a vintage personal shopper, this has been the most rewarding element of what I do. If I got a pound every time a customer reluctantly tried on a garment which turned out to be amazing, then I could probably retire or have a wardrobe full of to die for vintage!! Have fun, expect the unexpected and shop with an open mind, as you never know what may turn up.

- If you are looking for specific items set up an alert on Ebay so you will be notified every time something comes up – for example I have a thing for Chanel inspired bouclé jackets so I have set an alert so I know when anything is listed so I don't miss out.

- Don't automatically ask for the "best price" most sellers know what pieces are worth and they have spent time sourcing, cleaning stock so it is just plain rude – once you get to know them and become a valued customer, they will probably offer it anyway!! Just because something is second-hand it doesn't mean it will be cheap – the quality of the fabric alone is worth money and very often to get a similar piece new you would be so much more expensive and you would be looking at designer prices.

"Vintage and sustainability are the most important subjects in fashion for the next five or 10 years." - Nicole Phelps, 2018 Director Vogue Runway.

CHAPTER 7

My favourite places to shop vintage.

This is just a small section of vintage, charity shops, I always recommend having a google when you are heading to a new town or city to see what each place has to offer.

On-line stores.

Ebay and Etsy are a great place to start – you can search for what you are looking for and sellers will always list the sizes and measurements of the garments they are selling and don't be afraid to ask them questions if you are not sure of something.

Kerry Taylor Auctions holds regular high-end sales and you can pick up some amazing beautifully made designer items.

Shrimpton Couture is not a cheap option as she sells the most fabulous designer vintage pieces but well worth taking a look for something really special.

Wild Daisy Vintage for 60s and 70s bobo chic

Lil_vintage_ for chic classics

Mad Seventies for great 70's pieces with a masculine edge

Fabulous Miss K store for trend led vintage

Bemuse

Wake Up Little Susie – specializing in lingere and nightwear

Goldthrift Vintage

a_curated_life_by_gwynnie

edit_0.1

Manifestwoman – classic vintage and pre-loved pieces

Timebomb vintage – for original pieces from the 30s - 60s

A virtual vintage Market – hold regular markets on Instagram so make sure you give them a follow as they have a wide selection of vintage sellers showcased on their feed.

If you are after quality second-hand designer items then try – Re_see Paris, Vesitaire, Hardly Ever Worn London, Grace and Ted, Designer Exchange, Rebelle

Bricks and Mortar shops

London - Brick Lane, Beyond Retro, Retro Mania, Portobello Market, Cornucopia, Blackout Vintage, Grays Antiques, Frock Me Fairs, Rokit, Circa Vintage, Triad charity shops but have some great vintage pieces too, Liberty and Selfridge's also have vintage concessions.

The rest of the UK:

Birmingham – Gladrags, Juice, Covet, Moseley Vintage and Retro Bizarre.

Brighton – Dolly, Harlequin Vintage and Rokit.

Margate - Peony Vintage and Madam Popoff Vintage.

Manchester - Origins at Oxfam, Pop Boutique and Bells Antiques.

Norwich and Norfolk - Sue Ryder Vintage, Norwich Market, Retreat Vintage, Gregory's Vintage Girl, Portobello East Coast (Halesworth) and Vegas Vintage (designer vintage pieces housed in a boutique hotel in Diss).

Edinburgh - Anderson's.

Europe:

Paris - Mamie Blue, Thank God I Am VIP, Didier Ludot, Mam'zelle Swing and La Mode Vintage.

Amsterdam - Laura Dols, Ree-Member and Lady Day.

USA:

The Way We Wore, Decades

New York – there are so many but here are just a few I suggest googling before you go!! The Family Jewels, The Break, New York Vintage, Ritual Vintage and What goes around comes around.

Author profile

Karen James-Welton aka Fabulous Miss K is a fashion stylist specializing in vintage, blogger, writer, fashion show co-ordinator and lifetime vintage wearer. She styles fashion editorials, writes for a number of publications on the subject on how to make vintage modern, presented a regular vintage series on Mustard TV. She produced her first vintage magazine in Dressed in late 2019 and is working on issue 2. Karen has made her career in the fashion industry working as a stylist and personal shopping in London, Paris and now her home Norwich where she now lives in a house full of vintage and collectables and her husband of 22 years who thankfully shares her passion for all things vintage.

Photo credits ETT Photography, Luminoso Studios and Kerry Curl.

Printed in Great Britain
by Amazon